Six Networking Strategies for Entrepreneurs

Networking 101 for new startups and first-time entrepreneurs

By: Matt Holmes

DEDICATION

This book is dedicated to the Colorado startup community for having an awesome "pay it forward" culture to help young entrepreneurs like myself.

TABLE OF CONTENTS

Unique Ways to Think About Networking

<u>Networking</u>. As a small business owner, you will either be excited to hear that word or you will shutter when you hear it. Many love to network. They love to get out and meet new people. They live to socialize. Others see a room full of people and want to run back home. They would rather be by themselves. However, shaking hands is essential to grow your business.

Here are some other ways to help you think about business networking to take some pressure off and allow you to meet new people and grow your business.

- Making new friends. Tell yourself that you are just going to make some new friends. This might help really shy people by taking some of the pressure off about their business. Just go to socialize. Talk about your business but don't push it.
- How much you can help people. Your business can help people so you should want to help as many people as possible. Spread the

word by just wanting to help people. Worry about the sale later, and focus on personal relationships first.

- New business opportunities. Remind yourself that every person you meet is a new potential business opportunity. You should try to meet as many people as possible.

- You never know who can help you. Besides being able to help others, you might need help that you didn't realize. Be sure to listen to others in case you need their help too!

Networking can be very scary for some people. It might help to think about it as if you are just going to make some new friends. Building personal relationships is how all of Colorado's most successful entrepreneurs flew to success on autopilot. Try to take the pressure off completely. Who knows? You might just end up growing your business anyway. You should also remind yourself that every person you meet is a new business opportunity. You might also meet some people that can help you too!

Rookie Networking Mistakes

Many people hate networking. They despise it so much that they miss out on great business opportunities. They also miss out on meeting a lot of great like-minded people who could really help them grow their business. If they simply got over their fears, they may reap the huge benefits of connecting with experts, mentors, and like minded-communities. However, when one begins networking, it's key to be careful and not make any rookie networking mistakes.

Here are some mistakes that small business owners and entrepreneurs should avoid.

- Not having business cards to hand out. It is very important that you have business cards at a networking event (yes, it still is important in 2015). You are going to meet people that you will want to talk to at a later time and if they have no way of getting in touch with you, you might miss out on a great opportunity. If you just try to take their number, it does not look as professional as handing them a business card. Maybe they want to research you more before scheduling a meeting.

- Handing business cards out to everyone that you see and talk to. Doing this makes you look very desperate. You should only hand out business cards to people that you can see yourself doing business with or if you are truly interested in getting to know someone. Another bad practice is handing out multiple business cards assuming that the person will refer you after just meeting you. My network is my most valuable asset, and I wouldn't be able to sustain it if I handed them someone's card I had just met.

- Not following up after an event. It is very important to follow-up after an event. When you say that you are going to call them or email them after an event, make sure that you follow through with your promise. You do not want to lose business because you forgot. Many people like to send a little card which tells them that it was nice to meet you. Email works nowadays, too, even if you don't have a specific ask. Add them on LinkedIn, or give them a specific compliment on their website.

Though networking can be scary, it is very important to grow your business with larger customers, strategic partnerships, and setting up a referral network. However, you need to avoid certain mistakes so that you do not look like a rookie. You should never go to an event without business cards. You should also not hand out your cards to everyone that you see and look desperate. You must never forget to follow-up, especially if you promised that you would!

The Handshake: 3 Things to Remember

Business is a game. In this game, there's something called "making a first impression." To make a good first impression, there are many things you can do, like wearing a nice suit or shaving. But the most important part of making a good first impression is handshakin. Unlike a suit or a clean haircut and shave, a good handshake can make a relationship, that later leads to a sale. But what makes a good handshake? Here are three things you need to remember.

Firm Grip

The first thing to remember when giving a good handshake is a firm grip. A firm grip shows that you're confident in yourself and in your abilities. A handshake that's too soft shows that you're not confident and weak in your abilities. A handshake that's too hard shows that you're not considerate of other people and probably means you also haven't washed your hands since last using the bathroom.

Eye Contact

The second thing to remember when giving a good handshake is to make eye contact. Eye contact shows to someone that you are attentive to his or her presence and that the meeting is important to you. This will go far in cementing your business relationship. If you don't make eye contact, it shows that you don't care about the relationship or that you're real shy. No one wants to hang out with you people.

Lean In

The final thing you need to remember when giving a good handshake is to slightly lean in with open body posture. You want to lean in just enough that it's noticeable. This is a subtle gesture that shows you're willing to go the extra mile for the other person. Wear your biggest smile and give a good genuine nod while they're speaking.

Big Networking Mistakes

Networking can be a very scary thing, and many people go about it all wrong. They make a lot of mistakes which look bad on them and their business.

Here are some networking mistakes that you need to avoid doing.

1. Forgetting to network online. Social media allows businesses (and people) to reach a lot of people that they could not reach years ago. Use it to your advantage, Shakers.

2. Focusing on handing out cards, and not remembering to take any cards. Networking involves giving and taking. You want to meet people and take their cards too. Take some notes on the back of someone's card to help you recall what they do and how you can help them.

3. Focusing on sales instead of meeting people and building relationships. If you're going to have any success, you're at networking events to meet people and build relationships. Not to try

to close your next deal with someone you just met. You want people to remember you and trust you. Then, perhaps, down the road when they need something, they think about you.

4. Not being professional. Not everyone goes to networking events and dresses professionally. Which is sometimes okay. You should always dress consistent or just a hint above any event that you go to. There are enough distractions when networking, don't let your dress add to it.

Why Handshakin' Matters

It's not just a cliche or in your head--your handshake gives strangers enough information about you to make a first impression, and you want that impression to be one that matters. What they perceive, though, might surprise you.

Academic research on the power of the handshake

An article from The Journal of Cognitive Neuroscience studied the effects on people who received a handshake versus people who were actively refused a handshake during business and social engagements. The purpose of the study, according to the study's authors, was to look at "the impact of affective body language on evaluative responses in social settings and the associated neural correlates" (2292). Basically, the researchers wanted to determine whether or not there is a direct correlation between body language, specifically a handshake, and an individual's perception of the host of a social or business engagement. Surprise, surprise, there is!

The social handshake

In social situations, the study concludes that "a handshake preceding social interaction enhanced the positive impact of approach and diminished the negative impact of avoidance behavior on the evaluation of social interaction" (2303). As a host, you want to make your guests feel welcome at your social event by offering a friendly handshake upon arrival. Offering physical contact in the form of a handshake gives the appearance of further social engagements and serves to counteract any negative impressions that have formed. In this situation, a handshake really does make a good first impression because it demonstrates that you are friendly and open to meeting your guests personally.

The business handshake

As far as business goes, offering a formal handshake when meeting someone led to more positive impressions than neglecting to shake hands. Offering a handshake increases "ratings for competence, interest in doing business, and trustworthiness" (2297). Is this because offering a handshake before a business meeting is so socially ingrained that something feels amiss in the absence of such a formal greeting? The study doesn't indicate this, or really offer any answers as to why handshakes have such an impact on our first impressions, but it seems like a worthwhile question.Regardless of the reasoning, the fact remains that offering a handshake before a business meeting has positive effects.

Does grip matter?

The study did not focus on the strength of the handshake. Contrary to our popular culture's insistence in a "firm handshake" as the be-all end-all marker of strength, it seems that the simple but important act of offering a handshake instead of shying away from one makes you seem approachable, engaging, trustworthy, and competent.

Must-Ask Questions While Networking

No matter where in life you are in the current moment, networking is vital to success. This comes from both maintaining the key connections made in the past and developing new ones along the way as well. In order to make the most of everyone in your contact listing, work to ensure you've asked these three questions recently to each of them. The circular nature of maintaining your network and building it will soon be obvious when you learn to ask these questions on a regular basis.

1. How Can I Best Help You?

By asking what benefit you can be to someone else, you are more likely to engage them, to teach them your benefits, and be known as someone who will work to add value to their business or lives. Even the librarian could use help carrying a stack of books from time to time, remember. Rather than focusing on what they can do for you, stressing that you want to be able to give back to them promotes you as a generous figure. And generosity is a characteristic that goes far with just about every other human out there. Boom. Serve others first.

2. What Ideas Do You Have for Me?

While this may seem like an open-ended question, the truth of the matter is that you can make it as specific as you like, when relating it to how the conversation has started. Would you like any feedback on what services you have provided for them, ways that you might have been able to improve how you've worked to help them? Perhaps that librarian you just carried books for has a suggestion of which book you should read next in order to learn more about marketing tools. Asking for the person on the other end of the conversation to offer you knowledge and insight shows trust, interest and engagement as well.

3. My Next Step Is... Any Referrals You Recommend?

Networks function best when they are always in a state of growth. Tell your connection what you are doing and what you are planning, and then be open to asking for help. The lead for a new job may be the librarian's best patron, for example, who has recently stated she needs a new Social

Media Guru or company. Express the next phase of your plan, and always work to learn about new experts, leads, and general connections in order to make the most of your networking capabilities.

Offering assistance, asking for feedback, and working to constantly meet new people are the keys to building a successful network.

Matt 'Handshakin' Holmes claims entrepreneurs succeed through immersion in an entrepreneurial *community,* gathering feedback with industry *experts*, and building relationships with world-class *mentors*. After half a decade living in Denver and over half a decade of launching startups, the Handshakin Video Series interviews Colorado's most successful entrepreneurs on how shaking hands and personal relationships played into their success. Headquartered in a city that Forbes calls the second best place to launch your startup, he also launched Colorado's first Startup Pre-accelerator and organizes Startup Denver. Colorado might be known as the best place for pot smoking, outdoorsy younger folks; but we pack a hard punch backed with the authority of uncountable successful startups.

With news sources like Business Insider predicting that 40% of the American workforce will be freelancers, contractors, and temporary workers by 2020, the average American should learn how to make their own money right now. There are many quality resources, tools, and expert advice out there and we want to organize and share it with aspiring entrepreneurs, enabling them to chase their dreams.

Visit us at www.handshakin.com, and join to our email list for more free books!

Notes:

Notes:

Notes:

Notes: